TELL ME WHY, TELL ME HOW

WHY DO BEARS HIBERNATE?

DARICE BAILER

 **Marshall Cavendish**
Benchmark
New York

Marshall Cavendish Benchmark
99 White Plains Rd.
Tarrytown, NY 10591-5502
www.marshallcavendish.us

Library of Congress Cataloging-in-Publication Data
Bailer, Darice.
Why do bears hibernate? / by Darice Bailer.
p. cm. — (Tell me why, tell me how)
Includes index.
Summary: "Provides comprehensive information on bears and the function of hibernating"—Provided by publisher.
ISBN 978-0-7614-3990-5
1. Bears—Hibernation—Juvenile literature. I. Title.

QL737.C27B33 2009
599.78'1565—dc22

2008041996

Photo Research by Candlepants Incorporated

Cover Photo: Johnny Johnson / Getty Images

The photographs in this book are used by permission and through the courtesy of:
Alamy Images: John E Marriott, 1; Zuzana Dolezalova, 6; Mark Hicken, 7. *Peter Arnold Inc.*: Wildlife, 4; Huetter, C., 23. *Corbis*: Atlantide Phototravel, 5; Keren Su, 13; Jenny E. Ross, 20; William Campbell/William Campbell, 25; Joe McDonald, 15. *Minden Pictures*: Gerry Ellis, 8; Kim Taylor, 10; Jim Brandenburg, 11; ZSSD, 12; Matthias Breiter, 18, 21; Suzi Eszterhas, 22, 16; Thomas Mangelsen, 24. *Animals_Animals Earth Scenes*: Zigmund Leszczynski, 9. *Photo Researchers Inc.*: Art Wolfe, 14. *Digital Railroad.net*: Peter Bisset, 19.

Editor: Joy Bean
Publisher: Michelle Bisson
Art Director: Anahid Hamparian
Series Designer: Alex Ferrari

Printed in Malaysia

1 3 5 6 4 2

CONTENTS

In the wintertime, animals struggle to find food. Plants stop growing and a layer of snow buries the grass, nuts, and berries they eat.

How Do Animals Cope with Winter?

In the Northern **Hemisphere**, winter is the coldest time of the year. The Sun sets early during the winter, and that makes daytime shorter and nighttime longer. For three months, starting in late November or early December, the air is the coldest it is all year. When the temperature turns freezing, rain turns to snow.

When winter comes, you do not have to worry about finding a warm place to

Most humans do not have to worry about keeping warm during the winter months. We can go inside and turn up the heat or sit by a fire to keep warm.

live. Your parents can turn up the heat in your home or build a fire in the fireplace. When you go outside, you can put on a winter jacket and some warm mittens. If you need food, you can buy it at a grocery store.

Bears have to search for their food. They eat both plants and animals. Brown bears eat berries, roots, nuts, insects, fish, and **rodents**.

When winter comes, it is very hard for bears to find the food they like to eat. Mice **burrow** underground. The tops of lakes and ponds freeze, and fish

Winter is hard on a lot of nature. Many plants die during the coldest months of the year.

swim deeper underwater. Some insects die, and some hide from the cold. Plants stop growing, too. Plants need the Sun to grow, and with less

Before winter arrives, squirrels gather nuts so they will have something to eat when food is scarce.

light, they turn brown and die.

So how do bears survive in the winter? When snow falls and food disappears, animals survive in one of three ways. One way is to **migrate**, or travel to a warmer place where food is available. Another way is to store food. Squirrels gather up extra nuts and bury them to eat when it is cold and they are hungry. The third way is to **hibernate** inside a cave or **den**. Hibernation is like taking a very long nap during winter. To hibernate means to sleep through the winter until spring.

The spectacled bear looks like it is wearing eyeglasses because of the colored fur around its eyes.

All Kinds of Bears

You have probably seen polar bears or giant panda bears at the zoo. But did you know that there are eight different kinds of bears in the world? Besides panda bears and polar bears, there are brown bears, American black bears, Asian black bears, sun bears, sloth bears, and spectacled bears.

All bears are **mammals** with long snouts, short tails, and stocky legs. They have four paws with claws on them. Their fur is black, brown, cinnamon, white, or beige. Bears are good climbers and swimmers, and they can run as fast as 35 miles (56 kilometers) per hour.

Sun bears have a yellow or white ring of fur around their necks which looks like the sun.

Most brown bears live alone, except when they are mating or raising cubs.

Bears live all over the world except Africa, Australia, and Antarctica. Most bears live in the Northern Hemisphere, or above the **equator**.

Brown bears are some of the biggest bears in the world. They live in the wilderness of North America, Europe, and Asia. Most of the brown bears that live in the United States are called grizzlies because their fur has silver or white tips. The word *grizzly* means "sprinkled or streaked with gray."

There are more American black bears than any other kind of bear. They are medium-sized bears. Despite their name, black bears are not always black. They can also be brown, cinnamon, beige, or even white with a tinge of blue. The bears are found as far south as northern Mexico and all the way north to the Arctic.

The American black bear has five sharp claws on each foot for climbing trees.

The Asian black bear has a white or cream patch on its chest. These bears are also called moon bears because the patch looks like a sliver of the moon. The bears live in forests throughout Asia, including Iran, Korea, and Japan.

Polar bears are the largest bears in the world. They live and hunt seals on arctic ice around the North Pole and in northern parts of Europe, Asia, and North America. Polar bears have a great sense of smell. They can smell a seal 20 miles

(32 km) away. And polar bears can swim as far as 40 to 50 miles (64 to 80 km) to catch one.

Giant pandas are black-and-white bears that live in forests in China. They are endangered animals, and there are only about 1,600 of them left in the world. Giant pandas like to eat **bamboo** leaves and stems and are a symbol of peace in China.

Spectacled bears live in the Andes mountains on the western coast of South America. They often have a light-colored fur ring around each eye that makes them look as if

Polar bears can travel far on land, or in water. They have a thick layer of blubber to help them stay warm in icy water. Their flat front feet act as good paddles.

they are wearing glasses, or **spectacles**. These shy little bears are the only bears found in South America and the Southern Hemisphere.

Sloth bears live in the grasslands and forests of India and Southeast Asia. These bears can suck ants and termites out of their nests for a good meal. They also love honey, which is why some people call them honey bears.

Sun bears are the smallest bears and live in Southeast Asia. They are black with large yellow or white crescents on their chests. Sometimes they are called dog bears because they look like dogs and bark when fighting.

Now I Know!

How many kinds of bears are there in the world?

Eight.

Panda bears are easily recognized because of their black and white fur. They chew bamboo for hours every day.

During the winter months, there is less food for bears to eat so many of them hibernate.

Light Sleepers versus Deep Sleepers

As you have learned, bears live in many parts of the world. Sun bears, brown bears, American and some Asian black bears will start to hibernate because there is not much food for them to eat during the winter.

While some bears do take a winter snooze, scientists think they hibernate differently than other animals. For instance, bears sleep, but they can wake easily. Other animals that hibernate, such as bats, are very deep sleepers.

Bats hibernate if they live in places that are cold in winter. They hibernate in caves, buildings, between rocks, and in hollow trees. They hang upside down with their tails or wings wrapped snugly around them.

Many types of bats hibernate during the winter months. They hang upside down from a cave ceiling.

Did you know that there is even a fish that hibernates? During winter, when lakes freeze over and food is hard to find, carp hibernate under mud.

What is the difference between a bear's hibernation and the hibernation of other animals? Bears wake up more easily because they are lighter sleepers. For example, female bears wake up to give birth to their cubs in January or February. In the middle of hibernation, mama bears give birth, lick their **cubs** clean, and help them nurse before going back to sleep. These new mamas can wake up in a hurry to protect their newborn cubs, too.

Warm weather can also rouse the bears. Bears can sleep for up to six or seven months without eating or drinking. They have been known, however, to wake up on a warm day and roam around outside the den looking for food.

Mother bears give birth to their cubs during hibernation. After it is born, a cub will stay in the hibernation den with its mother.

Bears usually stay warmer than other animals that hibernate while they sleep. Maybe it is because their bodies are so big that they can stay warm more easily. The body temperature of a black bear during hibernation is about 88 degrees Fahrenheit (31 degrees Celsius). That is very close to a bear's normal temperature of 101 °F (38 °C). Because bears stay warm, they can wake up quickly to protect themselves or their cubs. On the other hand, it takes a couple of hours for other hibernating animals to wake up, warm up, and get moving. Some other animals have body temperatures that go down to just above freezing when they hibernate.

When a woodchuck is moving around, its heart might beat eighty times a minute. When it hibernates, its heart slows way down to just four or five beats per minute. The woodchuck's breathing slows until it almost stops. A hibernating woodchuck uses very little **energy**.

A bear's heart rate does not slow down as much as that. Neither does its breathing. A bear's heart rate might slow from fifty-five beats a minute to ten beats a minute.

This is the opening to a
polar bear's hibernation den.

Bears—the Best Hibernators of All!

Bears are the largest animals to hibernate. And some scientists call bears the best hibernators of all. For instance, bears do not go to the bathroom while they are hibernating. Instead, their urine is **recycled** and reabsorbed into their blood to make protein to keep their muscles strong.

Bears also have a special substance that makes them good hibernators. There is a **chemical** in the blood of every

A black bear looks out from its winter den dug into the ground.

hibernating animal called **hibernation induction trigger**, or HIT for short. Scientists say that HIT tells the animal that winter is coming and that it is time to go to sleep. When scientists draw a little blood from a hibernating animal and **inject** it into another animal, the other animal falls asleep. Even during summer!

Pregnant polar bears also have HIT, which tells them when to hibernate. They are the only polar bears that hibernate. They gain a lot of weight before they go into their dens in October. They give birth in November or December.

Two newborn polar bear cubs cuddle close together in their den to stay warm.

Pregnant polar bears need to be fat so that their cubs will be born healthy. If they are too thin, their babies might be too small when they are born. Also, the mother bears might not have enough milk to feed them if she is not properly fattened up.

A three-month-old polar bear cub looks takes a peek out of its den.

It is important for all hibernating bears to gain as much weight as they can during the spring, summer, and fall. And they do. Some bears gain 40 pounds (18 kilograms) a week! They grow a thick layer of fat to keep them warm during the winter. They also grow a nice, warm fur coat.

When spring arrives, a hibernating bear and its cubs will come out of its den.

How Bears Hibernate

All bears do not hibernate for the same length of time. Black bears that live in Minnesota, for example, will hibernate for about six or seven months. Winters last a long time there. But bears that live in North Carolina will hibernate for fewer months. Spring comes earlier there.

Other bears do not need to hibernate. They live in warm places and can find food all year round. For example, giant panda bears can find bamboo stalks to eat even during winter.

Sloth and spectacled bears do not hibernate because they live in warm places, too. Sloth

The spectacled bear does not hibernate because it lives in a warm climate where there is always food to be eaten.

bears do go inside caves to escape heavy rains during monsoon season, though. The monsoons, or heavy winds, last from July through September.

Some Asian black bears hibernate while others stay awake. It depends on where the bears live and how cold it gets.

In the fall, bears that will hibernate scour the woods for a good sleeping den. Bears like to make their dens in caves, on hillsides, under tree roots, or inside hollow trees. They want to be safe from wind, ice, snow, and **predators**.

Grizzly bears might spend weeks digging out a cave with their claws. When the den is just the right size, grizzlies gather up dried leaves, grasses, moss, and branches to make a soft bed.

Bears crawl inside their dens

Bears that hibernate during the winter will fatten up before they go to sleep, while there is still plenty of food available.

when it starts to snow or food disappears. Hibernating grizzlies might go into their caves or dens in early October. They will cuddle up and go to sleep, sometimes until April or May. They make it through the winter without eating by living off their stored fat. Their bodies break down this fat and use it for energy.

Pregnant polar bears scoop out ice and snow to make an underground den where they can stay warm and safe.

After hibernating, a grizzly bear emerges from its den thin and hungry.

Now I Know!

For how long do some American black bears hibernate?

Six or seven months.

When spring comes, hibernating bears wake up and are very hungry! They go outside the cave or den to look for a good meal. Spring is also the time of year when bears look for mates.

Female bears will give birth next winter, during hibernation. Their cubs stay with their mother until the second or third summer. They hibernate with her. Then, one day they are big enough to make their own dens. And they will go to sleep and hibernate—all by themselves.

# Activity

Bears around the world need your help. People are chopping down forests for wood and paper. Our planet is growing warmer, and the ice on which polar bears live is breaking up and melting. Sometimes they have to swim a long way to find seals. Sometimes they grow tired and drown.

Here are some ways that you can help save bears:

1. Save energy. Turn off lights, the TV, and your computer when you are done. Power plants burn coal and oil to make electricity. Smoke rises and a gas called carbon dioxide collects in the atmosphere. There it and other gases form an invisible lid. The lid traps heat, and Earth grows warmer. As Earth gets warmer, the polar bears' icy environment continues to melt.

2. Use less paper and use both sides of each piece before you recycle it. Dry your hands on cloth towels instead of using paper ones.

3. Use less plastic and paper bags. Buy cloth bags that you can reuse. Americans use 10 billion paper bags a year and throw away more than 100 billion plastic bags.

4. Ask your mom and dad to buy only eggs in that are sold in cardboard boxes. Styrofoam remains in garbage dumps forever.

5. Ride your bike when you can. Cars release harmful carbon dioxide in the air.

6. Plant flowers and trees. The green leaves remove the carbon dioxide from the air. They soak up carbon dioxide, mix it with water from the plant roots and turn it into oxygen.

7. Do not use weed or bug sprays on your lawn. These are filled with harmful chemicals that poison streams, lakes, and oceans.

# Glossary

bamboo—Woody grass.

burrow—A tunnel or hole in the ground that is used as an animal's home.

chemical—Something that is used to produce or make something else.

cub—A young mammal, such as a bear.

den—A shelter for a bear or a wild animal.

energy—The strength to do things.

equator—An imaginary line around the middle of our planet. It divides Earth in two parts halfway between the North and South Poles.

hemisphere—One half of a sphere or ball. It often refers to the northern and southern halves of Earth.

hibernate—To sleep through the winter when it's very cold and food is hard to find.

Hibernation Induction Trigger (HIT) —A substance found in the blood of hibernating animals that tells them that it's time to hibernate.

inject—To stick in.

mammal—A warm-blooded living thing with hair or fur that nurses its babies with its own milk. People are mammals and so are bears.

migrate—To move from one place to another when the temperature is low and food is hard to find.

predator—An animal that hunts or eats other animals.

recycled—Something that is used over again.

rodent—Small mammals with sharp teeth such as mice, rats, squirrels, chipmunks, and beavers.

spectacles—Eyeglasses.

# Find Out More

BOOKS

Bergen, Lara. *The Polar Bears' Home: A Story about Global Warming.* New York: Little Simon, 2008.

Englar, Mary. *Why Do Bears Sleep All Winter?* Mankato, MN: Capstone Press, 2007.

Guiberson, Brenda Z. *Ice Bears.* New York: Henry Holt and Co., 2008.

Hall, Margaret. *Hibernation.* Mankato, MN: Capstone Press, 2007.

Haywood, Karen. *Bears* (Endangered!) New York: Benchmark Books, 2008.

Salas, Laura Purdie. *Do Polar Bears Snooze in Hollow Trees?: A Book about Animal Hibernation* (Animals All Around). Mankato, MN: Picture Window Books, 2006.

WEBSITES

Defenders of Wildlife
www.defenders.org.

National Geographic Animals
www.kids.nationalgeographic.com/Animals/

The San Diego Zoo
www.sandiegozoo.org

North American Bear Center
www.bear.org/website

Index

Page numbers in **boldface** are illustrations.